W9-ARU-966

# If you were me and lived in...
# AUSTRALIA

## A Child's Introduction to Cultures Around the World

Carole P. Roman

Dedicated to my new friends Julie Gerber from Away We Go Media and  Bianca Schulze The Children's Book Review

*'Alone we can do so little; together we can do so much.'*

Helen Keller

Copyright © 2013 Carole P. Roman

All rights reserved.

ISBN: 1490522395

ISBN 13:  9781490522395

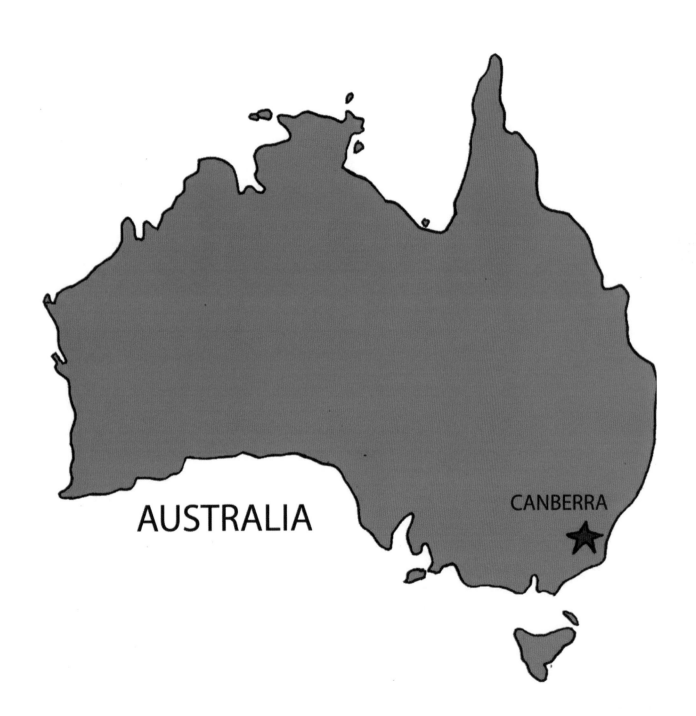

If you were me and lived in Australia (aw-strayl-ya), you would live in the Southern Hemisphere. The country is actually called the Commonwealth of Australia. The name "Australia" comes from Latin and means "south". People who live there are called "Aussies." (aw-cees).

Australia is not only a country, but a continent as well. A continent is a large land mass separated by oceans.

You might live in the capital city, Canberra (can-bruh). This is a picture of the Old Parliament house where laws were made until 1988. Canberra is located between two of Australia's most populated cities, Melbourne (mel-burn) and Sydney (s-Ih-d-nee). It was chosen as the capital city to make everybody happy. It is surrounded by a lot of vegetation, so it is called the "bush capital."

If you are a boy, you might be called Jack (J-ae-k), William (Will-yum), or Oliver (Oh-l-ee-v-EH-r). Favorite girls names are Charlotte (sh-AH-r-l-uh-t), Ruby (R-OO-b-y), and Sophie (So-fee).

You would call your mommy, "mummy" (m-uh-mee) and your dad would answer to "daddy" (Da-dee), just like in America.

When you go shopping with mummy,
you would use an Australian dollar.

If you were me and had a choice of what to do in Australia, you most certainly would visit the Great Barrier (ba-ree-ya) Reef. It's the largest reef in the world and can be seen from outer space. It is populated with brilliantly colored fish and jewel-colored coral. Dolphins, turtles, and whales make their homes there, too. You could get right up close to see them if you went snorkeling. Instead, you may like a ride in a bareboat, which is a mini submarine with windows

You would always pack a special lunch of vegemite (veg-gi-mait) sandwiches. Your mummy would spread this dark brown vegetable paste onto white bread with some Western Star butter. For dinner at home, daddy would roast meat on the barbie (bar-bee) which is another way to say barbeque grill. It is served with lots of fresh salad.

You and your friends would love to play cricket (crick-it), an outdoor game played on a large grass field with balls, bats, and two wickets (wick-its),which are posts that serve as goals. You would need eleven players to make a full team.

If you were me and lived *down under*, January 26th would be a special day. Australia Day celebrates when the British came to live and work in here in 1788. *Down under* is the way Aussies refer to their home because of its location on the globe. You would be proud to join the parades, eat many different foods, and attend all the events. If January seems like a cold time of year for a Parade, *no worries*, as they say in Australia— here in the Southern Hemisphere, January is the middle of summer!

18

You would love to go to primary school to learn all about Australia's many cultures. People native to Australia have lived on this large island for over forty thousand years. Australia was isolated from the rest of the world, so as a result the native culture remained rich and unchanged until Europeans arrived in the 1700's.

So you see, if you were me, how life in Australia could really be.

# Pronounciation

Aussies (aw-cees) nickname for Australians.

Australia (aw-strayl-ya) country in the Southern Hemisphere.

Barbie (bar-bee) barbeque.

Barrier (ba-ree-ya) large reef under the sea.

Canberra (can-bruh) capital of Australia.

Charlotte (Sh-Ah-r-l-uh-t) popular girls name.

Cricket (crick-it) a type of ball game.

Daddy (da-dee) Daddy.

Jack (J-ae-K) popular boys name.

Melbourne (mel-burn) large city in Australia.

Mummy (m-um-mee) Mommy.

Oliver (Oh-l-ee-v-er-r) popular boys name.

Ruby (R-oo-b-ee) popular girls name.

Sophie (So-fee) popular girls name.

Sydney(s-IH-d-nee) large city in Australia.

Vegemite (veg-gi-mait) a sandwich spread.

Wickets (wick-ets) goal posts in the game of Cricket.

William (Wii-yum) popular boys name.